Page 9:
You cannot *illegible* — divine Mind,

We Knew Mary Baker Eddy

MARY BAKER EDDY

We Knew Mary Baker Eddy

THIRD SERIES

The Christian Science Publishing Society
Boston, Massachusetts, U. S. A.

FOREWORD

In this third volume of the series "We Knew Mary Baker Eddy," as in those preceding it, The Christian Science Board of Directors is endeavoring to bring added knowledge of the great love her early followers had for Mary Baker Eddy, shown in loyal service to her. The reminiscences contained in this new volume are typical of the great appreciation and interest on the part of those who had the privilege of serving her, whatever the demands made upon them. The loyalty and affection which these faithful workers had for their Leader and the movement which she established are indicative of the steadfastness and devotion felt by them in carrying out her directions, for they knew that her directing was the result of prayerful thought and revelation.

I was one of the first to become acquainted with Calvin C. Hill upon his arrival in Boston. We were comparatively young, and it was quite usual for me, and sometimes two or three other young men, to meet at Mr. Hill's room in the evening, read the Lesson-Sermon, and have a chat about Christian Science. Soon I became aware of Mr. Hill's integrity and honesty, his devotion to the Cause of Christian Science, and his love for Mrs. Eddy.

Mr. Hill was a faithful student of the Bible and of "Science and Health with Key to the Scriptures," the Christian Science textbook. One could be with him for only a few minutes before he would substantiate some statement he made by quoting from the Bible or Science and Health, or from both books. In fact, one rarely got an expression from him which was not substantiated by a reference to these books.

Soon after coming to Boston, Mr. Hill found employment in a store, the principal business of which was the sale of carpets, rugs, and so forth. Mrs. Eddy learned of him in this capacity, and she evidently discerned in him the qualities which I have mentioned. His opportunities for serving Mrs. Eddy increased, as did his singleness of purpose to be of help to her.

At Mrs. Eddy's request Mr. Hill served her in several ways, such as confidential messenger between her and her Board of Directors. Mr. Hill strictly kept confidences. Because of his frankness, one was never in doubt as to what he thought. His loving service to Mrs. Eddy and to the Cause of Christian Science was increasingly evident.

As his friend through many years, I observed his faithful work for the Cause of Christian Science in the capacity of teacher and practitioner, in both of which offices there was always readiness to serve with loving and tender understanding.

I had the privilege also of observing the helpful activities of Mrs. Annie M. Knott over a period of years. During my long service with her as a member of The Christian Science Board of Directors I became intimately aware of her spirituality and her singleness of purpose in connection with the work of the Christian Science movement. She never swerved from what she believed to be a right leading in seeking the solution of any problem, and always strove to express through her strong character the spirit of the Christ. The Cause of Christian Science was greatly blessed by the faithful work of this very loyal and courageous woman. All of us who knew her had a deep and lasting respect and love for Mrs. Knott.

GEORGE WENDELL ADAMS

Boston, Massachusetts

July 1, 1953

CONTENTS

ILLUSTRATIONS

Some Precious Memories of Mary Baker Eddy

Calvin C. Hill

Compiled by

Frances Thompson Hill

MY early religious training at home and in the Presbyterian church prepared me to accept and appreciate Christian Science when it was presented to me in an hour of great need. Two of my brothers and two sisters had passed on because of tuberculosis, and I was filled with fear that I too might be a victim, for I was manifesting symptoms of the disease. The following is part of my testimony which was published in the August 22, 1903, issue of the *Christian Science Sentinel:*

In 1890 I gave up business in the East and went to try the high, dry climate of Colorado. I had been told that this was the only thing that would do me any permanent good. During eight years prior to this time I had been taking medicine for several diseases with but temporary relief. In 1892, Christian Science was presented to me by a fellow-salesman who had been healed by reading Science and Health. For three years I refused to listen to any great extent to what was said to me by this friend as to what Christian Science could do for me. In 1895, however, having given the climate as well as new *materia medica* remedies almost five years' trial without any lasting benefit, I decided to give Christian Science a trial, and did so.

That which was causing me most distress when I turned to Christian Science for healing was indigestion, for which medical treatment had been unavailing. I was healed of this malady in the first Christian Science treatment I received, and later all of my other infirmities and fears were dispelled by the light of Truth and Love as revealed in the Christian Science textbook, "Science and Health with Key to the Scriptures" by Mary Baker Eddy.

Naturally I wished to learn all I could about this wonderful spiritual truth which had so abundantly blessed me. I studied the textbook earnestly, and when the friend who had presented Christian Science to me said that he and his wife were moving to Boston in order to be at headquarters and render all possible service to the Cause of Christian Science, I decided to go to Boston at once where I could see Christian Science and Christian Scientists at work.

This was early in 1895. Upon my arrival in Boston I obtained a position with an excellent firm dealing in carpets and draperies. Soon after this I met members of The Christian Science Board of Directors and other students of Mrs. Eddy.

The more I studied Mrs. Eddy's writings, together with the Bible, and the more I heard Christian Science discussed by its adherents and saw it exemplified in their daily lives, the more convinced I became that it was what Christ Jesus knew, taught, and proved in many wonderful works of healing. In spite of this, however, I was prejudiced against Mrs. Eddy, as will be seen in the following excerpt from my testimony:

After coming to Boston, I began at once to attend the Mother Church services. At first I found much fault with the testimonies given at the weekly evening meetings, especially when Mrs. Eddy was referred to. My thought toward her had been poisoned by reading articles in the newspapers, magazines, etc., detrimental to her and to Christian Science. I was healed of this attitude of thought toward Mrs. Eddy, however, just as quickly and effectually as I was healed of dyspepsia, when one evening one of Mrs. Eddy's own students arose in the meeting and said in part, "You can no more separate Mrs. Eddy from

[3]

Science and Health than you can Moses from the Commandments, or Jesus from the Sermon on the Mount."

These statements healed me of my wrong thought toward Mrs. Eddy. With this healing I began to grow in the understanding of the teachings of Christian Science.

I have received great help from the *study* of the Bible and Mrs. Eddy's writings. "God is no respecter of persons." The promise is: "Seek, and ye shall find."

I am continually seeing in Mrs. Eddy's life the exemplification of her writings. Her life is proof to me that "one with God is a majority."

From the time of this awakening to a true estimate of Mrs. Eddy, I sought diligently to find her in her writings.

On Sunday, January 5, 1896, I had the inestimable privilege of being in The Mother Church when Mrs. Eddy came from her home at Pleasant View, Concord, New Hampshire, to give the Communion address. When the service had proceeded nearly to the point where the address was to be delivered, Mrs. Eddy entered the auditorium and walked down the aisle toward the rostrum. When she appeared the members of the congregation rose and remained standing until she was seated. After listening to the solo, Mrs. Eddy stepped forward, and in a voice resonant with spiritual power and beauty, and with articulation so distinct that not a syllable was lost, she gave the Communion address, which all may now read on pages 120–125 of "Miscellaneous Writings."

A well-known feature writer, Miss Lilian Whiting, was present at this service, and her description of Mrs. Eddy was published in the *Chicago Inter-Ocean*. It read as follows:

Mrs. Eddy is over seventy, yet her whole appearance is of a woman hardly more than half that age. She retains her delicacy of complexion, with its transparent clearness and brilliant flush; her dark eyes are bright, her graceful figure might be that of a girl of twenty, and her whole bearing is full of energy and charm. Her hair is white, which is almost the only mark that time has made upon her. Her presence is one of great dignity, of beautiful repose, of infinite sweetness. . . . A most remarkable figure in contemporary life is Mary Baker Eddy.

My first meeting with Mrs. Eddy came about in connection with the firm where I was employed, John H. Pray and Sons Company of Boston. On a Saturday in April, 1899, Mrs. Laura Sargent, a member of Mrs. Eddy's household, and James A.

Neal, already a well-known worker in Christian Science, came to the store to select samples of floor coverings for Pleasant View, Mrs. Eddy's home in Concord, New Hampshire. After they had made their selections and had departed, I found that we lacked sufficient yardage of some of the material. Also I believed that something more suitable for Mrs. Eddy's home could be obtained. The following day I went to New York, and early on Monday morning I made further selections of carpeting which seemed to me more appropriate. On Tuesday morning I took these samples to Concord.

I well remember that bright, spring morning. On arriving at Pleasant View, Mrs. Sargent received me and showed me to the back parlor, where I arranged the samples. I had barely time to glance around at the general color scheme and furnishings when the members of the household began to gather. While we were chatting pleasantly Mrs. Eddy entered the room.

I am often asked how I felt on meeting Mrs. Eddy for the first time. I can truthfully say that

I felt no strangeness. People are what their thoughts are, and I already knew many of Mrs. Eddy's thoughts. I had become acquainted with them through her writings.

Characteristically, I did not notice what Mrs. Eddy was wearing. I was aware of her erect carriage and dignity but much more aware of a sweet motherliness. I thought of my own mother, the noblest character I had hitherto known.

As I rose and took her outstretched hand I felt her swift, appraising glance. By that straight-through look I knew that Mrs. Eddy had read my thought and had taken my measure.

"This is indeed a privilege I have often wished for but never really expected to have," I said, "and I have brought you a little souvenir." It was indeed a *little* souvenir, nothing more than a memorandum book which my firm was distributing to customers. Mrs. Eddy accepted it as graciously as if it were a costly gift. Then, to my surprise, she turned to her maid saying, "Lydia, have you that little box I asked you to bring?"

"Here it is, Mother," she replied.

Mrs. Eddy handed me the box saying, "And I have brought you something." I opened the box and there was one of the silver souvenir spoons which had been made available to Christian Scientists the previous December.* These spoons bear a motto, "Not matter but Mind satisfieth," and to this motto is attached a story related to me by Calvin A. Frye, Mrs. Eddy's long-standing faithful secretary.

Early one cold winter morning in 1898, Mrs. Eddy called Mr. Frye and told him that during the night many wonderful thoughts had come to her. She talked about this for some time, then said, "Please write down this statement: Not matter but Mind satisfieth." Mr. Frye wrote the words on a slip of paper, but, he said, unlike his usual care in promptly filing all Mrs. Eddy's dictation, he laid the paper down and thought no more about it.

The following summer the head of a jewelry firm in Concord called on Mrs. Eddy one day and

* Later Mrs. Eddy gave me one of these spoons in gold.

proposed a design for what he called a "Christian Science souvenir spoon." Mrs. Eddy was much interested. Suddenly she exclaimed, "Wait a moment. I have just what is needed." Then she rang for Mr. Frye and asked him to bring her the slip of paper on which he had written the statement she had dictated to him during the winter.

Mr. Frye said that for a moment he was panic-stricken, for he realized that he had neglected to file that paper. He left the room not knowing where to look for it, but instantly the thought came: "Animal magnetism cannot make me the instrument for losing one word that God has given Mrs. Eddy. The same divine Mind that gave Mother that message protects it and will lead me to it." He was guided to go to the room where Mrs. Eddy had dictated the message and straight to the table drawer. There it was, the slip of paper with the message, "Not matter but Mind satisfieth," written in pencil. In telling this story Mr. Frye always added, "Mother never knew of the panic I was in when I could not recall where I had put that message!"

Of course I was delighted to receive this gift from Mrs. Eddy, and said, "I do thank you very much," adding frankly, "but I have one of these souvenir spoons already."

"Then you won't want this one," Mrs. Eddy said with a smile.

"Oh, yes, indeed I will, and I thank you very much," I hastened to assure her as I put the little box in my pocket. We all smiled broadly. We seemed very much like a large happy family.

I then proceeded to show the carpet samples, and Mrs. Eddy requested each one present whose room was to be recarpeted, to make his or her selection.

"Laura, choose what you would like for your room," she said, turning to Mrs. Sargent.

"You choose for me, Mother," Mrs. Sargent replied.

"Calvin, make your selection," she said to Mr. Frye.

"No, Mother, you make it," he responded.

Mrs. Eddy went through the same procedure

with each one present. Frequently she turned to me saying, "What would be your choice, Mr. Hill?"

Each time I would answer, "I should choose the one I like best, Mother," and Mrs. Eddy would say, "That is exactly what I shall do."

After I had stated three or four times that I should choose the carpet that I liked best, Mrs. Eddy shook her finger at me, saying, "But you have not yet said which one *you* would choose."

At that moment I learned that Mrs. Eddy did not like evasive answers; she liked positiveness. She had asked me a straightforward question which called for a straightforward answer, and I, unhesitatingly, gave her a very frank reply which was about as follows:

"In your front parlor, Mrs. Eddy, you have very fine Brussels net curtains, beautifully upholstered chairs, and a couch with a delicate covering; but in this rear parlor you have black walnut furniture with portieres and wallpaper which do not go together very well. A fine quality plain carpet, green or old rose, would look well in these double parlors. On the walls you should have the best paper that money can buy, and it would also be nice to have new window curtains."

With intensity I added: "One who has done so much for humanity should have the best of everything. Nothing is too good for you."

I was gesticulating as I talked, and Mrs. Eddy's alert gaze followed wherever I pointed. When I finished speaking she gently replied, "You know I do not go shopping very often so that I do not know much about the styles."

Of course I did not intend to be critical of Mrs. Eddy's home, which was in shining order. But I felt it was only right to give an honest opinion when she had asked for it, and I expressed myself as best I could. Later I had the privilege of helping Mrs. Eddy in the work of redecoration.

After we had finished selecting the carpets, Mrs. Eddy's thought quickly turned from the problems of her household to her larger household, the Cause.

Turning to me she said suddenly, "Have you seen the little heart?" Not knowing what she meant, I shook my head. "You must come to my study and see it," she said emphatically.

I followed her to the foot of the stairs, and she motioned me to precede her. I hurried up expecting her to follow more slowly. However, when I reached the top of the stairs she was right behind me. The newspapers were constantly referring to Mrs. Eddy's age; she was at this time in her seventy-eighth year. I realized that I had unwittingly accepted the suggestion of waning strength, but none was apparent. Leading to a door, she stood aside while I opened it for her, and we entered her study, the room over the back parlor.

In the center of the room stood an oak table and on it an inverted glass bowl. Under this I saw a piece of paper on which was glued a rubber band in the shape of a heart. After we were seated, Mrs. Eddy related to me what that rubber band, forming a heart, meant to her.

I was able to follow her explanation in a measure, because I knew that at this time an attempt was being made by some of her students who did not understand her to discredit her as Leader. It was a crucial hour for the Cause.

Mrs. Eddy told me that one night when she was waiting on God for a message concerning this problem, she took up a sheaf of papers to look through them, and put on her wrist the rubber band that bound them. Later, as she was pacing the floor in prayer, she tossed the rubber band on a chest of drawers. She noticed that it fell in the exact shape of a heart.

It was characteristic of Mrs. Eddy to find "sermons in stones," and the smile of God in a rose. This shape of a heart which a rubber band sometimes takes symbolized for her, in that trying moment, the great heart of God, "the ever-presence of ministering Love" (Science and Health, p. 567). She was assured that God had guided her to a right decision and that His plan would prevail, and she was comforted. Immediately she sat down and wrote this beautiful poem, "Signs of the Heart," which closes with a prayer that the "barren brood" might be awakened to the joy of each finding his own God-appointed place and that the dove of peace might rest and abide with them all.

SIGNS OF THE HEART

COME to me, joys of heaven!
   Breathe through the summer air
A balm—the long-lost leaven
   Dissolving death, despair!
     O little heart,
     To me thou art
A sign that never can depart.

Come to me, peace on earth!
   From out life's billowy sea,—
A wave of welcome birth,—
   The Life that lives in Thee!
     O Love divine,
     This heart of Thine
Is all I need to comfort mine.

Come when the shadows fall,
   And night grows deeply dark;
The barren brood, O call
   With song of morning lark;
     And from above,
     Dear heart of Love,
Send us thy white-winged dove.

This poem written in April, 1899, appeared in *The Christian Science Journal* of July, 1899. Later it was included in her published poems (Poems, p. 24).

That our Leader's prayer was answered is attested by a letter from the First Members of The Mother Church written June the third, and printed in the same issue of *The Christian Science Journal* in which the poem appeared. This letter shows clearly that these students understood the symbolism of the heart. It read as follows:

To our beloved Mother in Israel: —

The First Members of the Mother Church in Semi-Annual Meeting assembled, thanking God that among the countless blessings bestowed upon us out of the rich storehouse of Infinite Love, we *know* that in you, our Leader, Guide, Friend, Counsellor, and Mother, we have our crowning blessing; because through you He has taught us of Himself—eternal Life and Love.

We desire, as best we know how, to express our deep and renewed appreciation of the wisdom, strength, and majesty of Truth as reflected through you, and the infinite tenderness of that love which bears and forbears, in its Christly purpose to redeem and save.

We desire, also, here and now, to place ourselves anew upon the altar of self-sacrifice on behalf of our sacred Cause, and to extend our deepest assurances of unflinching desire and purpose to support you in every way possible to us in this, your hour of seeming persecution, *but of great blessing.*

As "them of old time" were guided, encouraged, and uplifted by trope, metaphor, and symbol, so are you, in this age, being shown the way whereby you and your children are drawn by the *band* of unity into the great *Heart* of Love.

We once again assure you of our supreme desire to love God and one another. We feel that persecution is but driving us nearer to God and to each other; and that the only *real* effect of malicious attack is to strengthen our courage and faith.

We know that you dwell constantly in the secret place of the Most High, because we believe the promises of God, and that "No weapon that is formed against thee shall prosper; and every tongue that shall rise against thee in judgment thou shalt condemn. This is the heritage of the servants of the Lord, and their righteousness is of me, saith the Lord."

Your loving children,

THE FIRST MEMBERS
OF THE MOTHER CHURCH

Boston, Mass., June 3, 1899.

The insight into Mrs. Eddy's problems as Founder and Leader of the Christian Science movement, and her way of solving these problems as it was shown to me in her explanation of "Signs of the Heart," touched me deeply. As she continued talking of ever-present Love, my thought was lifted into the upper chamber of Spirit's reality and allness through the door of spiritual illumination—understanding.

She then asked me many questions, evidently testing my grasp of Christian Science. My answers were based on what I had gleaned from her writings. Finally in a flash of apparent satisfaction with one of my answers, she said, "By the way, who is your teacher?"

"Well, Mrs. — Mother,"* I replied, "I believe I shall have to call you my teacher. I have been studying your book, Science and Health, and your other writings for the past four years, and if what is said to me by one of your own students or by one of your students' students is not backed up or verified by your writings, I take no stock in his statements, none whatever!"

Mrs. Eddy stepped forward, placed her hand on my shoulder and patted it gently, saying, "My child, my child, my child, you're safe, you're safe, you're safe!"

---

* Mrs. Eddy was called "Mother" by students and members of her household at that time. So it was quite natural for me, hearing "Mother" so often that day, to use the same term at our very first meeting. I can honestly say that I have always thought of her as Mother, from the first day I met her. Later Mrs. Eddy asked the students of Christian Science to discontinue calling her Mother.

Pleasant View, Concord, New Hampshire

As I saw it then and as I understand it more fully now, Mrs. Eddy meant that one is safe as long as he depends solely on divine Principle as revealed in her writings. She then asked: "Why didn't I know you when I taught my last class? I would have had you in it." Pausing a moment she continued, "But it was a Normal class." With a smile, a twinkle in her eye, and a decisive shake of her head, she concluded, "But I would have had you ready!"

I have no doubt that Mrs. Eddy discerned my honesty of purpose, my sincere desire to do my part with her guidance to help her and the Cause.

She then inquired if I had any questions I wished to ask her, but I was so impressed with her purity and greatness and my own impurity and unworthiness and I was so filled with emotion that the tears were running down my cheeks, and I could only reply in a trembling voice, "No, Mother." I was aware that I was in the presence of the Discoverer and Founder of Christian Science—the woman who, like Jesus, perceived the reality and allness of Spirit and the utter unreality and nothingness of matter, and who brought to mankind the Comforter of which he spoke.

Concerning this, Mrs. Eddy writes in her textbook, "Science and Health with Key to the Scriptures" (p. 55):

> In the words of St. John: "He shall give you another Comforter, that he may abide with you *forever*." This Comforter I understand to be Divine Science.

Of her inseparability from Christian Science, she has given us this explanation in "Miscellaneous Writings" (p. 105):

> Christian Science is my only ideal; and the individual and his ideal can never be severed. If either is misunderstood or maligned, it eclipses the other with the shadow cast by this error.

Mrs. Eddy then asked me if I had ever seen where she was born and led me out on the rear veranda which ran the full width of the house. Pointing straight ahead she said, "Right over that big tree, in the distance, are the Bow Hills where they say I was born." She paused and looked at me, or rather looked through me with that searching gaze which I later came to know so well. Then, instantly directing thought to man's spiritual nature and origin, she added, as I recall it, "But I wasn't, I was born in Mind." The gaze which followed that statement made an impression on me which can never be erased. I realized that she was speaking of her immortal, spiritual identity—that identity to which she clearly pointed in a letter written several years later to a clergyman:

> Should I give myself the pleasant pastime of seeing your personal self, or give you the opportunity of seeing mine, you would not see me thus, for I am not there. I have risen to look and wait and watch and pray for the spirit of Truth that leadeth away from person—from body to Soul, even to the true image and likeness of God. St. John found Christ, Truth, in the Word which *is* God. We look for the sainted Revelator in his writings, and there we find him. Those who look for me in person, or elsewhere than in my writings, lose me instead of find me (The First Church of Christ, Scientist, and Miscellany, pp. 119, 120).

As we were returning to her study I said, "There *is* a question I should like to ask you, Mother." She turned to me at once saying eagerly, "What is it, dear?"

Calvin Frye, who had joined us, said, "Be seated, Mother; be seated, Mr. Hill." In a few moments he withdrew and Mrs. Eddy again looked at me searchingly as I put my question.

"I wish you would point me to some place in your book that will enable me to overcome the thought of lust and sensuality." She replied most emphatically, "I will!"

I remember she lifted her head with that far-off look, as though she saw into the very heart of heaven. She talked for some time denouncing the Adam-dream and thoroughly exposing its falsity. She spoke over and over again of the nothingness of mortality and of the reality of the spiritual creation. She supplanted the garment of flesh with the robe of Spirit. The light which dawned upon me that day has dwelt with me in greater or lesser degree ever since and has enabled me to understand her revelation better as the years pass. She talked as long as I could follow her; but when she saw that her statements were beyond what I was capable of understanding, extending her hand, she said quietly,

"That will be all today, dear." This characteristic gesture, concluding our interview when I had ceased to follow her explanations, was to become very familiar in the near future.

As I left Pleasant View to return to the depot, after this memorable and uplifting experience, I felt as if I were walking on air. Nothing seemed real except the truth which Mrs. Eddy had affirmed and which was inscribed on the disc of my consciousness. People were passing in different directions, both on foot and in carriages, but I was scarcely aware of them—they seemed to be moving in a mist.

I boarded the train for Boston, and as I rode along, my thought was completely occupied with the great illumination of the reality of Spirit and the nothingness of matter. I felt that I had been lifted to the mount of transfiguration. For a number of days all I could think of, all I could hear, was what Mrs. Eddy had said to me in answer to my question, and the spiritual light which I received during that interview remained with me in all its glory.

From that time I was a different man; hence I feel warranted in saying that I experienced a measure of spiritual "new birth" on that wonderful day. However, later I had to learn that being lifted up by another, even by our Leader, is not working out one's own salvation; which is to say that there is no vicarious atonement. I saw that I had to work my own way up the hill of Science, that I had to prove in my own experience the truth she had affirmed to me,—I had to work it out in demonstration.

A month later I received a letter from Mr. Frye in which he said that he did not know why Mother requested it, but that she said to ask me to look on page 95, second paragraph, of Science and Health. In the fifty-fifth edition, 1891, then current, this read as follows:

The devotion of mortal mind to some achievement makes its accomplishment possible. Exceptions only confirm this rule, proving that failure is occasioned by a too feeble sense of power.

In the final edition of the textbook, page 199, these lines were changed to read:

The devotion of thought to an honest achievement

makes the achievement possible. Exceptions only confirm this rule, proving that failure is occasioned by a too feeble faith.

From Mr. Frye's letter I understood that Mrs. Eddy was continuing to help me along the road in Christian Science. The following letter from her shows that she remembered my first interview with her and that she was eager to give me further light on a problem which everyone must meet and master:

Goodness such as yours is a sure pre-text of success in all struggles to be "better." If a single sin remains—and who is destitute of all sin—be of good cheer for the victory over it is a foregone conclusion. If a supposed sensation exists that God, Good, is displeased with it must yield and neither fear nor abnormal conditions can hold it. Your good heart is the victor over it and *now* and for ever you know this is truth and the Truth has made you *free*. You are liberated by divine Love from every false claim of the flesh. The law of Spirit is supreme, it dominates the flesh and you are God's own child. *Never* born of the flesh nor subject to it.

Here you plant your understanding and having done your part, *stand* and God will provide for the temptation strength to overcome it.

About a month after my first interview I had the privilege of a second interview with Mrs. Eddy, when I was in Concord on a short vacation. I was staying at the cottage on the Pleasant View estate with Joseph Mann and his sister Pauline, with whom I had lived in Boston. I noticed that some of the workers on the estate were trying to burn a huge pile of brush, mostly apple tree prunings, but they had poured kerosene on the branches without having built a good foundation and the green stuff would not burn.

Recalling how I had seen it done on my father's farm when I was a boy, I said laughingly, "Let me show you how to burn brush." The task was willingly turned over to me. I borrowed a pair of overalls and a work shirt and set about laying a good foundation of dry pieces. Soon the flames were leaping up. In the midst of this burning of brush, Pauline called to me from the cottage window, "Mr. Hill, Mother wants to see you right away."

I hurriedly washed up, changed into my own clothes and went to the house. Mrs. Eddy was awaiting me in the library. She greeted me graciously and motioned for me to be seated. As I did so I began twirling the end of my moustache excitedly, wondering what she was going to say to me. "Mr. Hill, what a pretty moustache you have," she remarked, perhaps desiring to put me at ease. She then came directly to the purpose of the interview.

"How are you getting along with that problem you asked me about when you were here last?"

"Mother," I replied, "I am not quite sure I understand just what you meant in your letter."

"What don't you understand, dear?"

"Well," I said, "you reminded me of your statement that 'the devotion of mortal mind to some achievement makes its accomplishment possible.' By this I understand that if one devotes his thought to any particular line of work he will accomplish something. But the second part of the citation, 'Exceptions only confirm this rule, proving that failure is occasioned by a too feeble sense of power,' I don't know that I understand this. Does it mean my too feeble sense of power in Christian Science?"

"You *do* understand! That is exactly what it means," Mrs. Eddy replied emphatically. At that moment I awakened as I had not before to realization of the spiritual power of the statements of scientific truth in Christian Science.

Mrs. Eddy then began to explain a number of important points in the teaching and practice of Christian Science. She talked for fully half an hour and again I felt the inspiration of her spirituality.

This second exalting experience, following so closely upon the first one, seemed a wonderful climax to my four years of earnest study of the Bible and Mrs. Eddy's writings. My gratitude for Christian Science and to its Leader was so deep that I longed to serve her and the Cause in every way possible.

I consider that the opportunities that almost immediately began to come to me were the outcome of my sincere desire to give my life to the Cause of Christian Science, and of my firm conviction of its healing power.

When I was living with Joseph Mann and his sister in Boston, before they moved to Pleasant View, Joseph told me of his first healing in Christian

Science. Owing to the fact that it was so valuable to me as evidence of the power of Truth and also because of Mrs. Eddy's personal interest in the case, I here give the account of it.

This healing was widely known at the time it occurred because it had been presented at a hearing of a Committee of Doctors and Druggists which was attempting, through legislation, to prevent the practice of Christian Science healing. The National Constitutional Liberty League of Boston and New York published a pamphlet which included The Christian Science Case as prepared by Judge Septimus J. Hanna, then Editor of *The Christian Science Journal.* In this report Joseph Mann's testimony appeared as follows:

"AFFIDAVIT.

"Commonwealth of Massachusetts, } ss.
    County of Suffolk.

"Joseph G. Mann, being duly sworn, on his oath states:

"In November, 1886, I was accidentally shot with a thirty-two calibre revolver, the ball entering the left breast near the nipple. I immediately became unconscious, was carried into the house and laid on the nearest bed. On our doctor's arrival the family were informed that I had received a fatal wound; indeed so serious did he consider the case that he felt unwilling to father its responsibility alone. Accordingly three more well known and eminent physicians were summoned post haste. One of these was known in the city whence he came as a skillful surgeon. All four are to-day in the field of practice and their standing is considered as good as any in the medical profession, and in the community in which they live they are known as honest men. They examined the wound closely and carefully and concluded it would be useless to probe for the ball for if they should attempt this, or in any way stir me, I would die on their hands. They further concluded, that judging from the excessive bleeding, both internally and externally, and the peculiar color of the blood, the ball had touched the heart, and was probably lodged in the pericardium.

"The doctors informed the family that they were

unable to stop the flow of blood, and should they attempt this from without, I would still bleed inwardly, and thus bleed to death.

"After a few hours they held a council in an adjoining room, and then told the family there was no hope, saying to father: 'Mr. Mann, we are sorry, but we can do nothing for your son.' In his sorrow and desperation father implored them to spare nothing that money might afford, send for any other help that might bring hope; but they said it would be useless.

"With this verdict the three departed. While our family physician still lingered he kept the family informed that I was gradually dying; the body was growing cold, and before he left the house the eyes were becoming set and the death perspiration stood on the forehead. As he went out he said to our grieving friends that death was so near, the pulse was scarcely perceptible. All human help had now left, and the last hope of the family went out with it. So sure were the doctors of my death that they themselves told our friends and relatives, by the way, that they would never see me again alive. Telegrams were written and held ready to spread the news that I was dead.

"In this last moment, Christian Science was providentially brought to our door. The family had never heard of this (to them) new method of healing and refused to admit the Scientist; for, as they said, they wanted no one to experiment on the dying whom the *doctors* had given up as hopeless.

"They were assured, however, that the patient should not be touched or given medicine; and that 'man's extremity has been (is) God's opportunity.' Within about fifteen minutes after Christian Science had been admitted into our house I began suddenly to grow warm again under its treatment. My breath was again revived and normal. I became conscious, opened my eyes and knew I should not die, but would live. That same evening I sat up in bed and ate a little steak and toast. The excruciating pain I had felt during intervals of consciousness while dying, was all gone and I was steadily and rapidly growing strong and well. Notwithstanding the great loss of blood, I was strong enough the next day to have my blood-saturated garments (which had dried during the night and had to be removed by cutting) exchanged for clean ones. Beyond washing the wound and body to cleanse them from the blood, no attention was given them. The doctors on hearing that I had not died, predicted that gangrene and other evils would yet set in, especially on account of the excessive internal bleeding, and this would certainly produce death. I however continued to improve. The same power that had brought me to this point of recovery, forestalled also the bad results which the M. D.'s expected. The second day I was out of bed and dressed the greater part of the time; and the third day found me up bright and early and about with the family as though the accident had never occurred.

"That our mourning had been turned into joy is true, indeed; and to prove to my many visitors that I was really healed and quite like myself again in so short a time, I took my part with the family in singing our familiar church hymns; all were agreed that my voice was strong and sound. Relatives who had come to attend the funeral rejoiced with me instead. The wound healed inwardly and outwardly without any apparent inflammation, swelling, or suppuration; and meanwhile, from the fourth day on, I walked out to visit friends, rode with the family in carriage and sleigh over rough roads, and in all kinds of weather without sustaining the slightest ill effects therefrom.

"Christian Science not only perfectly healed me after the medical doctors had failed and had given me up, but through what understanding I have gained, I have ever since been kept well. When I was first healed I experienced a little soreness during the first few weeks of my being about, but this soon entirely disappeared, and not a sensation from the wound have I felt since.

"In the village which bears witness to my healing, is the home of my father, John F. Mann, where he has resided for upwards of forty years. I have no doubt that he, or any honest man, who was a citizen of Broad Brook, town of East Windsor, Hartford

Co., Conn., where my healing occurred, will give his testimony to any reader who might wish further evidence than my statement of it.

"Any who would personally inquire into this case are kindly invited to call on me at 418 Columbus avenue, Boston, Mass.

"Joseph G. Mann.

"Subscribed and sworn to before me this 27th day of February, A. D. 1894.

(Seal) "Walter L. Church, *Notary Public.*"

At the time of the healing related in the foregoing affidavit, Mr. Mann was twenty-two years of age. When the physicians gave their verdict that death was inevitable, the grief of the family was intensified by the fact that it was a brother-in-law who had accidentally shot him when the two young men were target-practicing with thirty-two calibre revolvers. When life returned the joy of the family was correspondingly great, and their gratitude for healing in Christian Science was profound. It turned three brothers and two sisters to active interest in Christian Science.

The first thing Joseph Mann said when he returned to consciousness was, "Is this something I can learn, and do for others?"

He immediately began to study the Christian Science textbook, and many, upon hearing of his healing, went to him for help, and he healed them.

When Mrs. Eddy was informed of his healing work she invited him to attend her class, which he did in 1888. Shortly after, he established his practice in Boston, and his sister Pauline joined him to keep his home. Ten years later, hearing of Mrs. Eddy's need for an overseer on her Pleasant View estate, he volunteered his services and left a growing practice in order to help her. In this same year Mrs. Eddy invited him to be a member of her last class, the well-known "class of seventy."

One day, when Mrs. Eddy was having a conversation with Joseph Mann, she questioned him in detail about his remarkable experience and especially about the regeneration which took place in him while he stood in the vestibule of death, a change which had come of an experience almost equal to his having died and then been resurrected.

Mrs. Eddy summarized the incident conclusively, I was told, in these words: "Joseph, you have had a *wonderful* experience; you were thrown violently out of the house, and picked yourself up on the outside; go not back into it."

My service to Mrs. Eddy began with making purchases for her and for members of her household. Soon she was entrusting me with messages to her Board of Directors in Boston. Later I served as Assistant to this Board. From this work there unfolded to me the opportunity, under Mrs. Eddy's direction, to find and recommend Christian Scientists to serve as helpers in her home. In 1901 I was appointed by our Leader as a First Member. [In 1903 the name "First Member" was changed to "Executive Member" and so continued until that body was dissolved in 1908.] In 1902 by unanimous vote of The Christian Science Board of Directors I was elected Superintendent of The Mother Church Sunday School, which office I held for fourteen years. Upon recommendation of Mrs. Eddy, in December of the same year, the Directors appointed me a member of the Finance Committee of The Mother Church. I served on this Committee for almost forty years.

The demands on Mrs. Eddy were so many that at times several secretaries were required to care for the correspondence. Resident secretaries and other workers necessitated a large household staff. The work of cook, waitress, housemaid, laundress, seamstress, and personal maid had to be done by sincere, unselfish Christian Scientists. All of those who were called to Pleasant View and employed there were experienced workers in Christian Science. Many had been Readers in branch churches, and some were teachers and practitioners. It was an inestimable privilege to live at Pleasant View and to be under the instruction and supervision of their Leader. In this connection Mrs. Eddy wrote in the *Christian Science Sentinel* of April 25, 1903: "It is true that loyal Christian Scientists, called to the home of the Discoverer and Founder of Christian

Science, can acquire in one year the Science that otherwise might cost them a half century" (Miscellany, p. 229).

Nevertheless, it was a constant problem for Mrs. Eddy to keep the staff of helpers she needed. Some who began their work with inspiration found it difficult to retain their joy and spiritual vision, especially if their assigned work seemed to be menial. Others could not continue because of strong home ties or for other personal reasons.

For more than two years I was assigned the whole task of finding helpers for Pleasant View. Then a committee was formed for this purpose, and I became a member of this committee.

In connection with this work Mrs. Eddy told me that in my quest for helpers I should go first to her own students—those who had received class instruction from her. She said that if such were physically fit they were the ones to serve in her home, because she knew what God had planted in their thought through her teaching, and at the proper time she could awaken that and make use of it. She said, "Get one who loves to work for the Cause and is willing to take up the cross for it as I have done." I knew that the qualities of thought required by our Leader in her helpers included love, orderliness, promptness, alertness, accuracy, truthfulness, fidelity, consecration, and humility. Mrs. Eddy commended me when, in one of my interviews with her, I said: "Mother, in looking for helpers for you, I am not trying to find a pleasant personality. I am looking for a quality of thought that reflects the great revelation you have given to the world." In her personal interviews with prospective helpers, I have known many cases in which she clearly discerned their thought and character at the first meeting. This evidenced her understanding of divine Mind. Mrs. Eddy knew immediately whether or not a person could qualify for membership in her household. There was never any question about it. I learned that she was always right, whatever I myself may have thought about the adaptability of a candidate. As I saw her great intuition and wisdom manifested again and again I came to the conviction that her judgment was as near perfection as is possible in this world.

One day when I was with Mrs. Eddy she rang for her personal maid and requested that she bring some article to her. The maid returned, bringing something totally different from what Mrs. Eddy had asked for. Mrs. Eddy looked at her earnestly and said, "Dear, that isn't what I told you to bring; I told you to bring [naming the article], and I told you where to find it. Now please get it."

Turning to me Mrs. Eddy remarked, as I recall her words, "That is what animal magnetism does to the members of my household, and they will say, 'Mother sometimes forgets!'" A few moments later Mrs. Eddy's ability to read thought accurately was again made apparent, for shortly after I left her I met the same maid in the hall, and she said to me, "Mother sometimes forgets what she asks for!"

In a letter to me Mrs. Eddy wrote: "We never can know who is in reality a Christian Scientist until he is tested under fire; then what is left are dregs unfit for use till purged and purified or they are qualities that evil cannot destroy and are held by the power of God." She further explained that in some cases the residue was mere sensuous, self-blind human will, whereas only the very opposite of this constitutes the individual, much more the Christian Scientist.

✗ On one occasion Mrs. Eddy said to me, in substance, "The first thing I do in the morning when I awake is to declare I shall have no other mind before divine Mind, and become fully conscious of this, and adhere to it throughout the entire day; then the evil cannot touch me." Many times she said to me, "All my hours are His."

Revealing the glory of her discovery, in a letter dated August 2, 1906, she wrote to me, " 'When first I learned my Lord' I was so sure of Truth, my faith so strong in Christian Science as I then discovered it, I had no struggle to meet; but stood on the height of its glory a crowned monarch triumphant over sin and death." Then, describing her own yielding to the divine demand, she spoke of her later experience in "Learning little by little the *allness* of

Omnipotent Mind; and the nothingness of matter, yea the absolute nothingness of *nothing* and the infinite somethingness of ALL." She added, "O bear with me, loved one, till I accomplish the height, the depth, the Horeb light of divine Life,—divine Love, divine health, holiness and immortality."

The work I was doing for Mrs. Eddy necessitated my being in frequent touch with her. Sometimes I saw her several times a week. On every occasion she expressed a loving interest in my welfare and gave a little of her valuable time to explain to me how to work in Christian Science. She read my thought as one reads an open book and discerned what I myself was unaware of, an unhealed fear of tuberculosis. She never talked to me of this, but in several of her letters to me she mentioned lungs. These excerpts were so helpful that I quote some of them in order that they may bless others.

In April, 1907, she wrote: "Dear one, look on the cloud of lungs till you see the Father's face—the sense of life not in nor of matter and this spiritual recognition will destroy the cloud forever, it *will*."

A few months later I received the following letter from her:

Pleasant View,
Concord, N. H.
Nov. 9, 1907.

My beloved: Read Science and Health page 188. ¶. 3. and may you get the meaning of what I said to you when last here.

It seems to the material senses that pain etc. are in the lungs or elsewhere *in matter* but the fact is that pain or suffering of any sort is no more in the body or matter in our waking state than it is in our *night dream* for *both* states are *dreams* and not the reality of being.

Lovingly yours,
M B Eddy

The following spring, in a letter, thanking me for some specially fine strawberries I had sent her, she said: "May, O may the Love divine feed you and fill you with a strong sense of *liberty*, of waking from the dream of life in lungs—the Infinite in the finite—and show you just how a lie destroys itself by saying I am real!"

Mrs. Eddy was deeply interested in the spiritual progress of her helpers and placed great value on their practice of Christian Science healing. She once said to me, as I recall it: "Get your heart right with the heart of God. That is what heals the sick. Get right yourself. Now, you get a practice and know that it is not you that heals, but that it is getting right yourself."

When I told her that I had decided to give up business in order to devote all my time, apart from serving her and the Cause, to the practice, she wrote:

> Pleasant View,
> Concord, N. H.
> March 2, 1903.

Beloved Student:

I am glad that you have left all, left but nothing for something, and this something *is All*.

God bless your brave, honest intent with its fullest fruition.

There are the sick the halt the blind to be healed. Is not this enough to be able to accomplish? Were I to name that which is most needed to be done of all else on earth— I should say heal the sick, cleanse the spotted despoiled mortal; and then you are being made whole and happy, and this is thine. "Well done good and faithful" enter thou into all worldly worth and the joy of thy Lord, the recompence of rightness. Again, God bless you, dear one, and guide your footsteps.

> With love,
> M B G EDDY

To
Calvin Frie

Pleasant View.
CONCORD, N. H. *Nov. 9, 1897.*

My beloved: Read
Science and Health
page 188. H. 3. and may
you get the meaning
of what I said to you
when last here.

It seems to the
material senses that
pain etc. are in
the lungs or else-
where in matter

But the fact is that pain or suffering of any sort is no more in the body or matter in our waking state than it is in our night dream for both states are dreams and not the reality of being.

Lovingly yours,

M B Eddy

Those who served Mrs. Eddy were blessed by the lovely grace of gratitude which she expressed. Gratitude was inherent in her nature and it unfailingly blossomed in some gracious way, a gift or a priceless statement of Truth—often with a delightful flash of humor, for she had a keen sense of humor.

On one of my early visits to Pleasant View, I noticed the chair Mrs. Eddy used regularly, an armchair upholstered in gold plush, was badly worn, and decided to surprise her with a new one. I had exact measurements taken and a reproduction made. One day while Mrs. Eddy was taking her drive I removed the old chair and put the new one in its place. With this gift I left a letter saying, "This chair is given to Mother with a sense of love and gratitude which cannot be expressed in words and my only desire is that it may give you the comfort that it does me the joy in giving it." In closing I thanked her for all she had done for me and for all mankind by her work and words. This gift delighted Mrs. Eddy, and she sent me a letter in which she quoted these lines from Eliza Cook's "The Old Arm-Chair,"

Mrs. Eddy's Study, Chestnut Hill, Massachusetts

To the left of desk is gold plush chair referred to on page 48

a poem very well known at that particular time:

> I love it, I love it! and who shall dare
> To chide me for loving that old arm-chair?

In this letter she enclosed a "card complimentary" to the Normal class of the Massachusetts Metaphysical College, which was to be held the following June.

This gift of a chair has a sequel. In 1907, when plans were being made for Mrs. Eddy's move from Pleasant View to Chestnut Hill, Massachusetts, one of my tasks was to have exact duplicates made of the oak furniture in her Pleasant View sitting room and bedroom. The reproductions were to be in mahogany, in light finish for the living room and in dark for her bedroom. One day when examining the furniture to be reproduced, I noted that the chair I had given to Mrs. Eddy in 1901 needed repairing and decided to have a duplicate of this made as a gift to her.

Recalling her letter of thanks in which she had quoted from "The Old Arm-Chair," I sent her the following note:

I would not dare chide you for loving your old arm-chair, but I have had made a duplicate of it so that you will not be the least inconvenienced while it is being repaired and made comfortable for you; then this new one can be placed in your new home when ready to be used until the other one can be forwarded. It is with much love and gratitude, and a sense of indebtedness to you which can never be repaid, that I present this gift with the hope that it may give you as much comfort as any earthly thing possibly can.

In her letter of thanks Mrs. Eddy spoke of the depths of her lone heart which seldom had company, and again referred to the poem, "The Old Arm-Chair," quoting the line, "I've bedewed it with tears, I've embalmed it with sighs." With her never-failing humor she added, "not size!"

I sent a little dish which I thought would be useful for her luncheon tray, and the next day I received the following letter:

Pleasant View,
Concord, N. H.
March 10, 1905

My dear Student:

You are more than a hill—you are a mountain, and the dwelling place of tenderness, unselfishness, Soul. The silver dish you sent me is very convenient to keep my lunch warm. Will you let me pay for it? I feel badly to have you expend your money for me. It is all I need and just what I do need to have you care for my needs, just as you are doing. God bless you, dear one, fill you with victory over the falsities of human thought and with sweet peace and rest from all fear. *Love* casts out fear.

Lovingly yours in Truth,
MARY BAKER EDDY.

Perhaps one of the most useful little gifts I gave Mrs. Eddy was a jewel box. She wrote me that it was always on her dressing case and that the compartments told her just where all her different things were to be found so that she could put her finger on them in the dark. In thanking me she wrote, "Order is essential to me." The letter closed with a benediction, "May heaven's rich blessings fall upon you as gently as dew upon the flowers."

One day Mrs. Eddy asked me to purchase suitable envelopes for her calling cards. She wrote on the back of one of the cards which she gave me, this treasured message, "With love untold to my faithful servant of God."

For the piazza at her Pleasant View home, I sent

her a rubber mat with the word "Eddy" worked into the design. In a letter acknowledging this she asked, "What shall I call it?" I replied, "Call that something on your doorstep a love gift for Mother and you will have the right name for it."

Mrs. Eddy's overflowing gratitude to her helpers was often expressed in charming gifts which we all treasured. In 1904 she sent me a twenty-dollar gold piece dated 1861 and with this a small reproduction of a photograph of herself which I placed in a little leather case and carried in my vest pocket. In a letter accompanying these gifts she wrote, "Accept my golden gift as the symbol of your Golden Rule of life." In thanking her for these, I wrote, referring to the photograph: "I have a better picture of you though than this one. It is a mental picture and was obtained by studying your writings. My desire is that the sunlight of Truth may fully develop this picture in my consciousness."

The following year she gave me a beautiful gold locket set with a diamond, containing another photo-

Gold Locket together with Reproduction of Photograph of Mary Baker Eddy

Referred to on pages 52 and 53

graph of herself. In acknowledging this I wrote in part:

I wish you could have seen my joyful surprise when I opened the box and looked upon the two faces—both solitaires, one with the lustre of, and symbolic of the light of faith and hope, the guiding star which led the wise men to where Jesus lay. The other with the lustre of, and reflecting spiritual being, growing brighter and brighter unto the perfect day because looking steadfastly upon the face of God, divine Love, symbolic of the light within— "the true Light, which lighteth every man that cometh into the world." I shall often look upon this face which reflects the Christ, to bring to memory my best and dearest earthly friend, the one who has followed unswervingly in the Master's footsteps, that I may receive renewed courage to continue in the way.

Mrs. Eddy loved to give books and she gave me several which she autographed. Most treasured of all is my copy of her textbook, "Science and Health with Key to the Scriptures."

In 1907 the so-called "Next Friends" launched a legal attack on Mrs. Eddy in an attempt to prove her incapable of taking care of her own affairs. Had these "Next Friends" succeeded in their purpose they would have obtained possession not only of her property but also of the copyright of Science and Health.

On March 24 of that year in a letter to me Mrs. Eddy said:

My beloved Student:

I beg that you will come to me March 26 or 27 to watch with me one or two weeks as the case may require.

This hour is going to test Christian Scientists and the fate of our Cause and they must not be found wanting. They must forget self and remember only their God and their Wayshower and their duty to have one God and love their neighbor as themselves. I see this clearly that the prosperity of our Cause hangs in this balance. May God open your eyes to see this and to come to her who has borne for you the burden in the heat of the day.

Similarly she appointed others, until there were twelve of us who were asked to do special work.

During the progress of the trial, I went to Pleasant View daily after each court session, carrying word to Mrs. Eddy from her chief counsel, Judge "General" Streeter, as to the progress of the case. She always received me at once, apparently waiting for me to come from the courtroom. I have a vivid picture of her, sitting quietly and listening to what

I had to report. She reminded me of a gray gull riding calmly, serenely, on a storm-tossed sea. She had full confidence in the triumph of Truth in this trial. As I recall, she once said to me, "You cannot hurt anyone by telling the truth, and no one can hurt you by telling a lie."

Of course I remember best of all the eventful day when I hurried out to Pleasant View and told her that the legal battle was ended—and that she had won. When she heard this she raised her hands from the arms of her chair and dropped them again, she lifted her head—a movement which had become familiar to all of us when she was doing metaphysical work or when she was deeply moved. Her eyes had a far-off look as if she were seeing the very heart of heaven.

Almost at once she turned to her desk and wrote for a few minutes. It was a letter of overflowing forgiveness to one of those in whose name the suit had been brought. I thought of Jesus' words, "Father, forgive them; for they know not what they do."

For my work in connection with this case Mrs. Eddy gave me directions which I immediately wrote down. She wanted the belief of "lawsuit" handled with absolute metaphysics. I was not to outline what the verdict would be but to know that Truth would prevail and that divine Mind would direct the verdict —which it certainly did.

My mental work was based on the Daily Prayer in the Manual and also on Article VIII, Section 6, "Alertness to Duty." Mrs. Eddy pointed out the need for specifically handling hypnotism in this case. She quoted from the Bible: "Shall not the Judge of all the earth do right?" (Genesis 18:25), "Surely the wrath of man shall praise thee: the remainder of wrath shalt thou restrain" (Psalm 76:10), and "We know that all things work together for good to them that love God" (Romans 8:28). In every detail her instruction was Christianly scientific.

Illustrating once more her ready wit, Mrs. Eddy wrote me shortly before the suit was won and signed her letter, "Your best friend, but not your next friend."

Some Precious Memories

Many times I have been asked to describe Mrs. Eddy. I recall her graceful form, her small hands and feet, her delicate rose coloring and white hair expressing the charm of a Dresden figure. Her face was almost unwrinkled, but there were crinkly lines of humor at the corners of her eyes. Her mouth showed firmness, but her smile was inexpressibly sweet. Her eyes were wonderful—deep, searching, far-seeing, but with often a merry twinkle. Her expression responded instantly to her thought. She had a quick sense of humor and in the midst of serious business had time for a word of wit or enjoyment of an amusing situation.

When those of us who were associated with Mrs. Eddy have given our recollections of her as a "corporeal person" (Miscellaneous Writings, p. 152), we come back to the fact that she can be truly known only through her work for God and humanity. She discovered the Science of Being. She proved it in healing and so made it practical for mankind. She systematized its teaching and so made it universally available. She gave the Church

Manual and thereby made her church secure against "the sacrilegious moth of time" (Miscellany, p. 230); she established this "eternal Science" as a "permanent dispensation" (Science and Health, p. 150).

Under the caption "Practise the Golden Rule" Mrs. Eddy wrote to the *Boston Globe* in 1905, "Through the wholesome chastisements of Love, nations are helped onward towards justice, righteousness, and peace, which are the landmarks of prosperity." And as though summarizing her own immortal achievement she adds, "In order to apprehend more, we must practise what we already know of the Golden Rule, which is to all mankind a light emitting light" (Miscellany, p. 282).

Through Mary Baker Eddy, God has given to humanity the complete, final revelation of Truth, divine Science.

Reminiscences of Mary Baker Eddy

Annie M. Knott

IN January, 1882, I came to Chicago, after four years spent in England, the greater part of that time having been in London. Soon thereafter someone I knew had treatment in Christian Science from one of the first students of Mary Baker Eddy in Chicago, and my friend was healed in a few days of a long-standing ailment. Nor was this all, for I was told that the claim was made that Christian Science was the method practiced by Christ Jesus and taught to his disciples. My comment was that if this were true there was nothing in the world worth troubling about. I soon found that it was true! Many cases of healing came to my notice, and as I began to study "Science and Health with Key to the Scriptures" by Mrs. Eddy, every sentence brought conviction as in the study of geometry, and proofs multiplied.

My first meeting with Mrs. Eddy was in February, 1887, when I had the privilege of studying in her Normal class. It was a very cold morning, and when I entered the College at 571 Columbus Avenue there were a number of other students removing their wraps and going upstairs to the classroom. As I did not expect to meet anyone whom I knew, I paid little attention to those who were coming in, but presently a very sweet voice greeted me by asking my name. In a moment I realized that I was in Mrs. Eddy's presence, and could scarcely find my voice as I thought upon the moral and spiritual greatness of the woman who was speaking to me. I gave my name, and then realized that she held my hand in her own with gentle pressure, and asked if I was not cold. I think I responded in the negative, although to the senses I was uncomfortably cold, but my thought was immediately lifted above the physical to the realization of that which I had been cherishing for a good while.

As I looked into Mrs. Eddy's face I saw at once the wonderful character expressed so far as the human face and form can express it. The graceful figure, the beautiful hands, the well-shaped head

Mary Baker Eddy

Reproduction of photograph given with gold piece
referred to on page 52

with its dignified poise, the masses of beautiful brown hair, which at that time showed no trace of gray, and above all the wonderful eyes, with the depths of thought and feeling which looked out beyond the human sense of things into spiritual realities. With all this flooding my consciousness I realized that Mrs. Eddy was no stranger to me, because for more than two years I had been learning to know her through her great message to humanity, "Science and Health with Key to the Scriptures." From the first hour almost that I had opened the book I was aware that it was for me a complete key to the Scriptures, and not only so, but I had proved through its teachings that Christian Science is indeed the promised Comforter, and that the healing work practiced by Jesus and taught to his disciples had become a present reality.

When I entered the classroom, students from different parts of the country were introducing themselves to each other, and in a few moments Mrs. Eddy herself entered and took her place at one end of the classroom. Here I ought to say that

I had scarcely left her presence to ascend the stairs when I was aware of a warm glow in my hands, and all sense of chilliness and discomfort had gone. Not only was this true, but in the classroom I could not help observing that my hands seemed to be changed, and the redness and roughness due to the cold outside had entirely vanished, nor did it ever return. This, however, was a small thing compared with the searching questions which opened up the thought of the students to the actual work of the class. On many occasions I have noticed Mrs. Eddy's remarkable keenness in observing the thought of those in her presence, and on this morning it gave me a never-to-be-forgotten lesson. ×

Mrs. Eddy had only spoken for a few moments when she evidently discerned mentally some thought not in line with Christian Science, and so she asked whether anyone in the class believed in what was known as spiritualism, or, to put it otherwise, believed that communications from those who had passed on were possible. In asking this she said that if any of those who were present did so believe, they might raise their hands. One lady who sat near me did so, and instead of a stern rebuke or criticism Mrs. Eddy smiled gently and said: "Thank you. Your honesty in responding to my question will be of much service to you in gaining a clearer sense of Truth in these lessons." Mrs. Eddy then asked her what was the basis for her belief in spiritualism. The lady at once responded that she had had evidence of it on several occasions, that she had had communications from her own mother, who had passed on some years before. Mrs. Eddy looked serious for a few moments, and then asked the student if she had not at times experienced sickness and suffering, perhaps even after becoming acquainted with the teachings of Christian Science. The lady admitted that she had had such experiences, and Mrs. Eddy went on to ask her if they did not seem very real indeed. To this the student responded in the affirmative, when Mrs. Eddy said in substance: The evidences of which you have spoken are on the same line with the sense evidence of disease and pain. Neither the one nor the other deals with spiritual reality, but only with varying phases of mortal belief.

The student then began to contend that the Bible gave a number of instances of communications from those who had passed on, and cited first the story of the witch of Endor. This was quickly disposed of, for Mrs. Eddy showed that it only represented a prevailing belief in spiritualism, that even Saul's edict that witches were to be put to death indicated a widespread belief in the necromancy of that day, and that when Saul, in his human extremity, turned away from God, he fell into the deep pit of superstition and disobedience to divine law, and lost the way of Truth. This was made so lucid by a few words from Mrs. Eddy that no argument was needed, but the student then offered the experience of Saul of Tarsus on his way to Damascus to persecute Jesus' followers. The student claimed that Jesus personally called to this man, better known to us as Paul, and so illumined his consciousness with truth that he was turned from his erring ways and began to be a follower of the Nazarene Teacher. Mrs.

Eddy expressed some surprise at this argument, and asked if any others in the class believed that this had been a personal appearance. Without waiting for an answer she called upon a member of the class who was seated in front of her chair, and asked how he regarded it. He spoke at some length and explained that before coming into Christian Science he had believed that it was the personal Jesus who addressed Paul, but that after studying "Science and Health with Key to the Scriptures," he had come to see that it was a subjective experience, that the eternal Christ spoke to Paul and wakened him from his erroneous thinking, and that while Paul probably continued for some time to think that it was the personal Jesus who had addressed him, nevertheless Christ Jesus became to him the Way-shower to Truth and Love. Mrs. Eddy commended the answer, and with a few kindly words to the student who had been the means of opening up this discussion, she went on with the regular teaching.

The following is a statement which Mrs. Eddy

made in class, and which was copied by Mr. Frye and given to the members of the class: "In treating against malpractice the student must not call the names of individuals because he cannot know who is sinning always but he can make sin to himself nothing through divine Science. Declare positively, mortal minds cannot harm me or my patients. One Mind governs all harmoniously." We were to declare daily, "I cannot suffer from others' sins for sin is its own punisher and I will not sin, then I am free from suffering."

The closing lesson followed on something of the same lines as the others, and for myself I could hardly say that it left me with a happy sense of the experiences which might come at any time. Within a few days, however, I was back at my work in Detroit, and was called upon to heal some more difficult cases than any I had before encountered in my two years' practice. I was even astonished at the results in these cases, and at this late day love to think upon the spiritual strength which had come to me from this teaching of our Leader.

The second day after my return I was called to treat a man who was said to be violently insane, so much so that three men had to be in the room with him all the time. The lady who came to ask me to take the case was not a Christian Scientist, nor were any of the family, but the case was so desperate that someone had suggested Christian Science treatment to them. I said to the lady who came for me that I could not possibly go to the case as I had some very important healing work at the time. The lady was greatly disturbed and said, "You call yourself a Christian woman and yet you refuse to come where the need is so great." I replied, "No, I cannot refuse if you put it on that basis. I will come as soon as possible."

When I reached the home three men were waiting in the hall downstairs to go up and relieve the others who were in the man's room, and I was told that it would not be possible for me to enter the room at all, that he would become so violent if he saw a stranger that he could not be held at all. I, however, was given a quiet room near him and remained for over a half hour. Mrs. Eddy's wonderful teaching in the recent class became so clear to me that I felt I could raise the dead if called upon to do so. After I left the room I was told that the man became calm and peaceful after my treatment began, although neither the man himself nor those in the room knew of my being in the house. He spoke to his son in a perfectly rational way and said he must have been very sick, and told the son to call his mother. The wife came up full of thankfulness and sat down beside him. The others were all asked to leave the room as there was no need of their services any longer. Although he had not been asleep for a week and drugs had failed to have any influence, he fell asleep and remained quiet for over twenty-four hours. When he waked up the next day he was disturbed for a short time, but I was hastily summoned to the house and again treated him with good results as on the first occasion. There was no return of this dread illness, and I never saw the man until a few years passed, when I saw him Sunday after Sunday in our Christian Science church.

Within a few weeks after the Normal class of February, 1887, I received a letter from Mrs. Eddy inviting me to be present at a meeting of students to be held April 13, of that year. When this request came I felt that I could not well spare the time or money to return to Boston so soon after I had been there, and wrote her to that effect. (I afterwards learned that the majority of those who had been asked to come on for this gathering had sent our Leader word that they would be unable to comply with her request, and some did not even take the trouble to notify her of their unreadiness to respond to her request.) Within a short time, when I was about to give treatment to a patient who had called, there was delivered to me by the American Express Company the following letter from Mrs. Eddy:

571 Columbus Ave.
Boston, March 31, 1887

My dear Student

I have gotten up this N. C. S. A. [National Christian Scientist Association] for you and the life of the Cause. I have something important to say to you, a message from God. Will you not meet this one request of your teacher and let *nothing* hinder it? If you do not I shall never make another to you and give up the struggle.

Lovingly Your Teacher

M B Eddy

It is needless to say that this message from our Leader dispelled the thought which was seeking to hinder students from responding to their teacher's request, and within a few minutes I was hastening to the Western Union office to wire Mrs. Eddy that I would without fail come to Boston as she had requested. This seemed to call for a sacrifice of time and money, but the experience has always been remembered as a vital step in my progress. Mrs. Eddy's address at the meeting of her students in Tremont Temple was wonderful, and the only regret I can ever feel in connection with the gathering is that it was not published, but only a few hints of it given in the *Journal*. I also learned on this occasion the lesson which we need to think upon many times, that simple obedience to any righteous requirement in our Cause brings unstinted reward. Throughout the year I did everything in my power to be ready for the gathering in Chicago in June, 1888. It was at this time, however, that I heard Mrs. Eddy declare that unless students of Christian Science waked up to the need of the hour, "this Truth would again be lost and buried beneath the rubbish of the centuries."

On the morning of April 14, 1887, I had the privilege of an interview with Mrs. Eddy at the College. This was more than I expected, and her words to me on that occasion made a deep impression upon my thought. Mrs. Eddy began the interview by asking me if I was clear on the great truth that God does not know evil, which she had sought to impress upon us in the Normal class of the previous February. I replied that I thought I did remember her teaching very distinctly, and then she went on to say: "If you stood in front of a mirror, and there was a hole in your dress or a pin in your dress, it would be in the reflection, would it not?" I answered, "Yes." She then said, "It would not be possible to get it out of the reflection so long as it was in the original, would it?" I answered, "No."

She said, "You are clear about this, are you?" I replied, "I think I am." She then went on: "Now God never changes, does He? He is eternally the same." To this I again responded, "Yes." She again went on, "Now if God were conscious of sickness, sin, and death, we could never expect to overcome them, for the divine consciousness does not change, and we could never remove from the reflection that which is in the original." She again asked me to answer her, which I did, seeing as I had never seen before the vital importance of gaining a clear sense of this truth. This was the substance of the interview, but I have thought of it many times in the years since then, as mortal mind puts up a tremendous argument that God must know evil in order to help us in overcoming it, whereas the opposite is the case.

This same day our Leader asked her students to meet with her at the College, and after talking to them for some time she gave them the privilege of asking her questions, to which no one responded. I myself for a long time regretted my silence on this occasion. Mrs. Eddy mentions this incident on page 137 of "Miscellaneous Writings."

I had the privilege of again seeing our dear Leader and listening to her words at the meeting in Chicago, June, 1888, of the National Christian Scientist Association. Two sessions were held in the First Methodist Church in Chicago, and these were attended only by Mrs. Eddy's own students or by others who had received class instruction from them, the teachers vouching for their own pupils. Mrs. Eddy herself was on the platform, and patiently answered the many questions which were asked from the floor in regard to the healing work, also to the relations of teachers and their students. Her answers always directed thought to the demands of Principle and the need for the maintenance and advance of our great Cause. Besides the sessions held by Mrs. Eddy for her students only, I listened to her wonderful address at the National Convention in Central Music Hall on June 14, which is to be found in "Miscellaneous Writings" under the title "Science and the Senses." To me it was wonderful beyond words, and with the passing of the years it seems no less so. I was, of course, present at the reception at the Palmer House on the evening of that day, and I may say that the reports of the meeting in Central Music Hall and also of the reception at the Palmer House were freely if not very correctly given by the Chicago papers, quoted in *The Christian Science Journal.* Nothing could, however, hinder the great spiritual awakening which came to all who attended these meetings from extending over the whole world, with the firm conviction that the Christ healing had come again through Christian Science. ✗

Mrs. Eddy speaks of these meetings in the article "Loyal Christian Scientists," which begins on page 275 of "Miscellaneous Writings." Toward the close of this article she says that she had been "gradually withdrawing from active membership in the Christian Scientist Association." To me it is beyond question that the work of the National Association had all been intended to prepare thought for the development of the Christian Science Church, which later was called The Mother Church, which, of course, includes all of its branches.

Mrs. Eddy early discovered that humanity needed not only to know God but needed a church. Moses knew this and accomplished wonders in the way of its establishment. To the Jewish people the Ten Commandments were undoubtedly the basis of all law and order, and we may rejoice that in the church which Mrs. Eddy established she emphasized the importance of the Decalogue in every way. In my own work most of the healing was brought about quickly, but those healed remained in their old churches because at that time we had not a church of our own in Detroit to which we could invite them; consequently those who were healed made little or no progress. Some, however, became students, and in attending the students' meetings they were made ready for withdrawing from their former churches, and for becoming members of the Church of Christ, Scientist. This, however, called for very earnest work not only in Boston but throughout the entire Field, yet it was more and more clearly seen that Christian Science churches alone could establish and maintain the Christ healing.

In October, 1888, Mrs. Eddy invited me to call on her at her home, 385 Commonwealth Avenue, and she spent over an hour with me, saying that I must begin to hold public services in Detroit and to preach sermons.

After this lengthy interview when I rose to leave, Mrs. Eddy took my hand and said, "Now, will you do what I have told you?" To which I replied that I would "try." To this Mrs. Eddy responded very firmly, "No, that is not enough. Will you *do* it?" And of course the only proper response was to say "Yes!" And Mrs. Eddy's closing words were, "Then, do not forget!" For a time after my return to Detroit I preached sermons in accordance with Mrs. Eddy's instructions. Many, however, of those who had become interested and were studying our textbook, "Science and Health with Key to the Scriptures," did not wish to leave their former churches, in some cases because of their families, but in reality they did not readily see what it meant to separate themselves from religious bodies who believed that man is material and governed by material law. Those, however, who were gaining the truth more quickly did not hesitate, but were willing to leave their families and attend Christian Science services. ✗

On October 5, 1892, I attended a meeting in Boston called for the purpose of carrying forward the organization of The Mother Church under its present form of government. The meeting was held in Steinert Hall, 62 Boylston Street, when fifty-seven persons signed the roll of membership, myself among them. At the close of the meeting I was quietly invited to visit Mrs. Eddy the next day at her home at Pleasant View, Concord, and I may add that my sister, Mrs. Isabella M. Stewart, C. S. D., of Toronto, was asked to accompany me on this trip.

We were made happy beyond words by this great privilege, and when we reached our Leader's home we met there six other Normal students who had come to share this blessing. As our dear Teacher entered the room we could not help being impressed by her grace and dignity, and the evidence of spiritual growth which is often more apparent than the physical growth of a child from year to year. While to the outward sense her hair had become white, evidence to us of the tremendous efforts called for in ascending the mount of revelation, the tone of the spiritual authority based on her wonderful understanding of Truth was the most impressive thing I for one had ever felt. She greeted us lovingly, then asked Mrs. Sargent to bring her Science and Health, which she did at once.

The students who were present listened earnestly while our beloved Leader read to us these impressive words from Science and Health (page 101 of the 70th edition, lines 19–24): "When we realize that there is but one Mind, the divine law of loving our neighbors as ourselves is unfolded to us; whereas a belief in many ruling minds hinders man's normal drift towards the one Mind, one God, and leads human thought into opposite channels, where selfishness reigns" (page 205 of the present edition). As she read this to us from our inspired textbook, it seemed as if those few lines alone furnished the rule for working out every human problem, no matter how difficult it might seem, and especially the marvelous words, "man's normal drift towards the one Mind, one God." Her wonderful understanding rang out in every word as she read this passage. She pointed out to us without hesitation, as Christ Jesus had done in his day, the attacks of error to which her followers would be subjected, but at the same time she reminded us constantly of the utter powerlessness of error to hinder the progress of Christian Science.

Toward the close of her remarks she said that we must never fear evil, no matter what the seeming might be. And then with a radiant smile, she added that her students thought too much about evil, and often in belief gave it too much power. She went on to say that when error knocks at the door, they sometimes open the door to see what it wants, but Mother did not do that; she knew in advance what it wanted and kept the door shut; but that after her students had opened the door, they had to get the intruder out, and the great thing was to keep error out. At the close of her remarks, before saying good-bye to us she said: "If you, my dear students, could but see the grandeur of your outlook, the infinitude of your hope, and the infinite capabilities of your being, you would do what? You would let error destroy itself." This statement has been passed out a good many times by some of those who were present on that occasion, with slight variations. I wrote it down in this form immediately on going back to the hotel where I was stopping. The interview lasted for nearly two hours, and to several of those who were present it seemed like a whole course of lessons.

At the close our dear Leader invited us to go upstairs with her and see her rooms, especially her study, and then she took us out on the balcony to see the fine view in every direction. One of the students present turned to her suddenly and said, "Mrs. Eddy. won't you point out to us the place where you were born?" To this Mrs. Eddy responded in her characteristic way, and with a

Birthplace of Mary Baker Eddy, Bow, New Hampshire

From an original engraving

radiant smile said, "Oh, I never was born, but if you mean Mary, well, Bow is over there," at the same time indicating with her finger the direction in which we could look to see what would humanly be called her birthplace.

Between 1890 and 1898 it was my duty to represent the Christian Scientists at the Michigan State Capitol in opposition to medical legislation which if enacted would have restricted the practice of Christian Science in the State. On one of these occasions I addressed the Legislature, declaring myself "a student of the Rev. Mary Baker Eddy, the Discoverer and Founder of Christian Science." The Legislature thereupon acted favorably to protect Christian Scientists in their constitutional right to religious freedom.

Some time after this when I was visiting Mrs. Eddy, I told her of this experience, and asked her if I did right in using her name and speaking of myself as her student when I addressed the Legislature, and she replied that I had done exactly right.

The following is in a letter which I received

from her, dated May 10, 1897, in regard to the great victory in the Legislature at this time:

She wrote: "Darling, 'Scots who hae wi Wallace bled'—have a moral force innate. Thank God, and my faithful Annie for this brave just defense of Christian Science."

During these years the Christian Science movement was advancing wonderfully, and in 1898 Mrs. Eddy established the Board of Lectureship, my own name being among the appointees.

In January, 1899, I was invited to see our Leader at Pleasant View, and had the inestimable privilege of a long interview with her. She asked how I was succeeding in the lecture work, and I told her I had had very few calls up to that time. I added that even personal friends who were members of Christian Science churches wrote me that while they would be glad to hear me, people in general preferred to have a man lecture for them, and so I was temporarily at least like a "briefless barrister." At this point Mrs. Eddy spoke in her usual energetic manner and said it would not do to let that argument stand, that she had appointed me after due consideration, and that it rested with me to make good. Her words were these: "You must rise to the altitude of true womanhood, and then the whole world will want you as it wants Mother." She said further, "I would like to know who has the most intellect, the man or the woman?" And then she laughingly added: "There is not any such thing as intellect, but I mean who reflects the most intelligence, the man or the woman? Take Adam and Eve, was it not the woman who first discovered that she was in error and was the first to admit it?" To me this was a new definition of intelligence, and I never lost sight of it. The result of her talk was indeed wonderful, for within a short time I began to have numerous calls to lecture, and, what is more, felt the inspiration of Truth to accept these fearlessly and to prove that a woman can declare the truth and heal the sick as well as a man.

On June 6, 1899, when Mrs. Eddy spoke in Tremont Temple, I was on the platform and had been asked to speak there, as I was a lecturer at that time. When Mrs. Eddy entered from the back of the platform we were all delighted, and the few words she spoke meant much to us. Lady Dunmore and her son Lord Fincastle were seated next to me.

I was among those who heard Mrs. Eddy speak from the balcony at Pleasant View in 1903. I also saw her in 1904 at the time when the cornerstone of the Concord church was laid, when she spoke a few words to Mr. Edward P. Bates, the President of The Mother Church, as she handed him a gavel to be used at the annual church meetings.

In June, 1903, another change came in my own work, when I was called on Mrs. Eddy's recommendation to become one of the editors of our periodicals.

A few months later I had the great privilege of another interview with Mrs. Eddy at Pleasant View, where I remained for a few days on her gracious invitation. Every minute spent in her presence meant so much because of her wonderful reflection of divine intelligence, and so I spoke very little, preferring to listen to her inspired words. One morning when I was a guest there she sent for me to come to her room on leaving the breakfast table, and when I entered it she said she wished to call my attention to a passage which she had just read, and which had come to her with new light. She opened the Bible and read from John 4:39–42, but laid the emphasis upon the 42d verse, which reads: "And said unto the woman, Now we believe, not because of thy saying: for we have heard him ourselves, and know that this is indeed the Christ, the Saviour of the world." She paused a moment and said, "I think I ought to call the other members of the household to receive this message," and this she did. As these students came into the room she repeated what she had said to me, and again read the verse mentioned. Looking very earnestly and lovingly at all of us she added, "You can each of you, I am sure, say this for yourselves, that you believe, not because of what I have told you, but because you have proved for yourselves that Christian Science is indeed 'the Christ, the Saviour of the world.'"

The Board of Directors and the editors were

summoned by telegram to meet Mrs. Eddy at Pleasant View at two o'clock in the afternoon of October 5, 1905. On our arrival we were shown to her study and took our seats in a semicircle in front of the chair where she usually sat, in the corner of the room. There were present Messrs. Chase, Johnson, Armstrong, Knapp, McLellan, Willis, and myself. After greeting us Mrs. Eddy addressed the Directors individually by name, and asked each one if he read carefully the *Journal* and *Sentinel*. Each one in turn said he did, but perhaps not so carefully as he ought to do. She then said quite gravely that she wanted them to read the periodicals with the utmost care, and to assist her in guarding them from any erroneous or misleading statements which might escape the notice of the editors.

She then took up from her desk a copy of the *Christian Science Sentinel* of September 30, 1905, and read these words from an article, "a diseased body is not acceptable to God." She read them without indicating in any way whether she approved or disapproved of them, then asked each of us if

we considered that statement scientific. I happened
to be the last of that group of seven persons, and
Mrs. Eddy again read the words already quoted,
and asked me if I considered the statement scientific.
I replied that I had stumbled over it twice, but had
decided to let it go through. Mrs. Eddy paused for
a moment and then said in tones I can never forget,
"Then you are the one to blame. You are my
student, are you not?" I responded, "Yes, Mrs.
Eddy, I have that great privilege." She then said,
"Did I ever teach you anything like this?" To this
I made no response, beginning to realize that a
serious mistake had been made. She then addressed
the whole group and said in strong tones, "Now,
will you any of you tell me whether God has any
more use for a well body than for a sick one?" This
came like a flash of light, and we all wondered at
our own dullness. Turning to me again she said
that her reason for having me come to Boston was
because she hoped I would have been able to see
that her teachings were strictly adhered to in the
articles which went out, and that I had failed to do

this in the statement in question. She insisted that man's likeness to God is never a physical likeness, and called our attention to page 313 of Science and Health, lines 12–19.

Then she turned to Science and Health and asked us to read daily for the present on page 295, lines 5 to 24. She turned to one of those present and said, "You sometimes believe, do you not, that you can see as well through a brick wall as through a window?" He respectfully replied that he hoped he did not, but she said it would sometimes appear as if he did because of what he wrote, and with her usual splendid dignity and yet great humility, she referred to herself as the transparency through which the light of Truth had come to our age, and speaking for myself I can only say that this means a thousand times more to me today, after the added years of experience, than it did when Mrs. Eddy talked with us.

Mrs. Eddy went on to speak of the work of Christ Jesus, and she said that she was sometimes troubled at the false concepts of the Master which occasionally found their way into the *Journal* and *Sentinel*, and turning to the editors she said very forcefully, "I do not want to see any more of those namby pamby concepts of Jesus go out through our periodicals to mislead people as to what he actually taught." She quoted some of his severe denunciations of the scribes and Pharisees, where he called them whited sepulchres, and so forth, and she added, "If I had said such severe things about those who have opposed Christian Science as he did to his opponents, I would have been put to death long ago."

Here it is only right to say that while I was deeply grieved to have caused our Leader disappointment, indeed sorrow, a rebuke from her was worth much more than the praise of others, and I took it gratefully. Mrs. Eddy talked with us for nearly two hours, and left it very clear that no one is to be judged by his or her physical condition, but by character and spiritual attainments.

Within a year of the time I became an editor, I was also appointed by Mrs. Eddy a member of the Bible Lesson Committee, which work I enjoyed greatly, and I remained a member of this committee until 1918. I have always felt that one of the most important parts of our Leader's divinely inspired instruction for the advancement of our Cause was the selecting of subjects for the Lesson-Sermons, and thus providing for the spiritual needs of humanity beyond the present hour and into the far future. As the years go by I see this more and more.

In 1919 I was called to be a member of The Christian Science Board of Directors, and while I shrank from the responsibilities involved in this forward step, it seemed that obedience was the need of the hour, and I at once responded.

INDEX

INDEX

Index

Index

Represents Christian Scientists at Michigan State Capitol, 1890–1898, 81
Appointed to Board of Lectureship, 1898, 82
Invited to visit Mrs. Eddy at Pleasant View, 1899, 82
On platform with Mrs. Eddy at Tremont Temple, June 6, 1899, 83
Hears Mrs. Eddy speak from balcony at Pleasant View, 1903, 84
Sees Mrs. Eddy at laying of cornerstone of Concord Church, 1904, 84
Becomes Assistant Editor of periodicals, 1903, 84
Interview with Mrs. Eddy at Pleasant View, 1903, 84
Summoned to Pleasant View, October 5, 1905, 85, 86
Appointed member of Bible Lesson Committee, 1906, 89
Called to be member of Board of Directors, 1919, 90

L

Leader, 14, 16, 17, 24, 28, 37, 38, 40, 66, 69, 70, 72, 73, 77, 78, 80, 82, 89, 90
Lesson-Sermons (See Christian Science Bible Lessons)
London, England, 59
Loyal Christian Scientists, 74

M

Mann, John F., 34
Mann, Joseph G., 26, 28, 29, 31, 35–37
Mann, Pauline, 26, 28, 36

Massachusetts Metaphysical College, 49, 60, 71, 72
McLellan, Archibald, 86
Methodist Church, 73
Michigan State Capitol, 81
Miscellaneous Writings, 5, 73, 74
quoted, 20, 57
Moses, 4, 75
Mother Church, The, 4, 16, 17, 75, 77, 84

N

National Christian Scientist Association, 69, 73, 74
National Constitutional Liberty League, 29
Neal, James A., 5
"Next Friends," 53
New York, 6

O

Old Arm-Chair, The (poem), 48–50

P

Palmer House, Chicago, 74
Paul, 64, 65
Pleasant View, Concord, 4, 6, 23, 26, 28, 36, 38, 39, 48, 49, 51, 54, 55, 77, 82, 84, 86
Poems
quoted, 15
Poems
Old Arm-Chair, The, 48–50
Signs of the Heart, 14, 15
Pray, John H., and Sons Company, 5
Presbyterian church, 1

S

Sargent, Mrs. Laura, 5, 6, 10, 78
Saul, 64

Index

Science and Health, 1, 2, 4, 18, 44, 53, 54, 59, 61, 65, 76, 78, 88
  quoted, 14, 20, 24, 25, 58, 78
Science and the Senses, 73
Sermon on the Mount, 4
Signs of the Heart (poem), 14, 15, 17
Steinert Hall, Boston, 77
Stewart, Mrs. Isabella M., 77

Streeter, Gen. Frank S., 54
Sunday School, The Mother Church, 37

T

Tremont Temple, 70, 83

W

Whiting, Lilian, 5
Willis, John B., 86